WITHDRAWN

 River Forest Public Library
735 Lathrop Avenue
River Forest, IL 60305
708-366-5205
October 2017

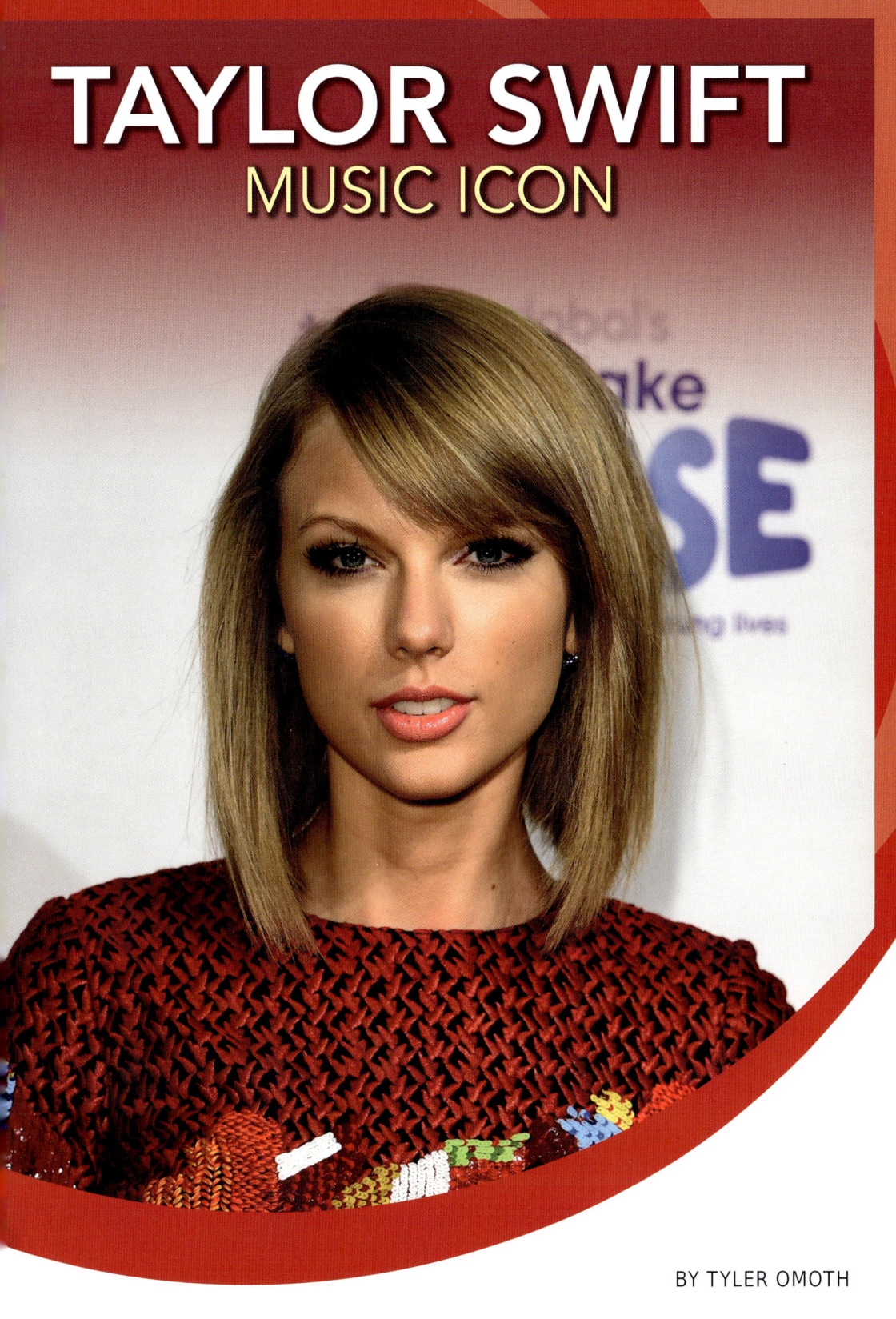

TAYLOR SWIFT
MUSIC ICON

BY TYLER OMOTH

Published by The Child's World®
1980 Lookout Drive • Mankato, MN 56003-1705
800-599-READ • www.childsworld.com

Photographs ©: Ian West/Press Association/URN:23356912/AP Images, cover, 1; Shutterstock Images, 5; Mark Humphrey/AP Images, 6, 14; S. Bukley/Shutterstock Images, 8; Jeff Christensen/AP Images, 10; Everett Collection/Shutterstock Images, 12; Jason DeCrow/AP Images, 16; Eric Jamison/Invision/AP Images, 18; Al Powers/Powers Imagery/Invision/AP Images, 20

Copyright © 2018 by The Child's World®
All rights reserved. No part of this book may be reproduced or utilized in any form or by any means without written permission from the publisher.

ISBN 9781503819993
LCCN 2016960923

Printed in the United States of America
PA02335

ABOUT THE AUTHOR

Tyler Omoth has written more than 30 books for kids, covering a wide variety of topics. He has also published poetry and award-winning short stories. He loves sports and new adventures. Tyler currently lives in sunny Brandon, Florida, with his wife, Mary.

TABLE OF CONTENTS

FAST FACTS 4

Chapter 1
PERSISTENCE 7

Chapter 2
A BIG BREAK 11

Chapter 3
A COUNTRY STARLET 15

Chapter 4
CROSSOVER TALENT 19

Think About It 21
Glossary 22
Source Notes 23
To Learn More 24
Index 24

FAST FACTS

Name
- Taylor Alison Swift. She is named after the singer James Taylor.

Birthdate
- December 13, 1989

Birthplace
- Reading, Pennsylvania

Nicknames
- Tay Tay, Tater Tot

Fun Trivia
- Taylor likes to cook. She tries out new recipes when she hosts dinner parties.
- Taylor has a fish tank filled with vintage baseballs in her home.
- In 2016, Taylor surprised a bride on her wedding day. She stopped by the wedding reception and sang "Blank Space."

Chapter 1

PERSISTENCE

For a moment, the room was silent. Taylor Swift's pulse was racing. She had just finished dancing on stage and belting out the lyrics to LeAnn Rimes's song "Big Deal" for a local talent competition in Strausstown, Pennsylvania. She lowered the microphone and looked out into the crowd. She was 11 years old. A smile blossomed on her face as the crowd before her burst into applause.

Taylor stepped off the stage. She waited in suspense as the votes were tallied. When it was announced that she had won the competition, Taylor couldn't believe her ears. Her prize was to be the opening act for a country music group, the Charlie Daniels Band.

◀ **Taylor Swift starting playing the guitar when she was 12 years old.**

▲ At the 2010 Grammy Awards, Taylor became the youngest singer to win Album of the Year.

Taylor quickly realized that she wanted to be a singer. She begged her mom to take her to Nashville, Tennessee. The music industry was booming there. Taylor knew if she was talented enough she could record a **demo** and land a record deal. When her parents agreed to take her to Nashville, Taylor couldn't stop smiling.

They visited many record companies, but Taylor had no takers. She continued to write songs and perform. She auditioned to play in a Songwriter's Showcase and was granted a chance to sing. Taylor stood on a small stage at Nashville's Bluebird Café, armed with only her guitar and her voice. She strummed the strings on her guitar. Taylor began playing one of her songs for the small crowd. Each chord vibrated throughout the room.

As Taylor performed, a man in the audience listened to the sound of her sweet and powerful voice. Taylor had caught the ear of Scott Borchetta, a record executive.

Once he heard Taylor sing, he knew he had found a star. Borchetta approached 15-year-old Taylor and gave her the chance of a lifetime. He wanted to sign her to his new company, Big Machine Records. From performing a simple **acoustic** set in a café, Taylor had just landed a record deal.

Chapter 2
A BIG BREAK

Taylor sat cross-legged on the floor with a notepad and a pencil. Her high school freshman year was coming to an end. The boy she was dating would be leaving for college soon. Taylor began to write him a song. As she wrote, she thought about her favorite things. She wanted him to remember their time together and smile. The words flowed onto the page and the song "Tim McGraw" was born.

"I started thinking about all the things that I knew would remind him of me. Surprisingly, the first thing that came to mind was that my favorite country artist is Tim McGraw," Taylor said.[1] As Taylor chased fame, this song remained on her mind.

◀ Taylor sang her song "Picture to Burn" at the 2008 CMT Music Awards.

▲ **Taylor traveled across the country during her Fearless Tour in 2009 and 2010.**

When she finally got the chance to record music, Taylor decided to play "Tim McGraw" once more. The song was released on her first **album** in 2006, titled *Taylor Swift*. Taylor began to hear her song drift out of radio speakers. It was a hit.

One year later, Taylor was invited to perform at the Academy of Country Music Awards.

A spotlight illuminated her blonde curls as she stood on stage. She tightly held her guitar and began singing "Tim McGraw" to the large room filled with country music artists and fans.

> "Anytime someone tells me that I can't do something, I want to do it more."[2]
>
> —*Taylor Swift*

As she sang, Taylor carefully walked down the stairs at the front of the stage. She moved toward the crowd and finished her song in front of a smiling Tim McGraw.

Taylor's voice caught the attention of the country music industry. Soon, Taylor was accepting awards for her music. In 2007, 18-year-old Taylor won the Country Music Association (CMA) Horizon Award. That same year, she also took home the Academy of Country Music Award for Top New Female Vocalist. Taylor was thrilled with her new success but she wondered if she could keep writing songs people loved.

Chapter 3

A COUNTRY STARLET

Heartbreak hit Taylor hard. She sat on the floor of her bedroom, crying over a boy she liked but couldn't be with. Her family and friends didn't like him. She grabbed a pen and notebook. Her tears hit the page as she wrote down lyrics to a new song. It was about forbidden love. She named it "Love Story."

The song was released on Taylor's second album, *Fearless*, in 2008. "Love Story" struck a chord with her audience. It soared to the top of the country music charts. For a time, it was the biggest selling **single** in country music history. "Songs happen in really weird, strange, quirky ways," Taylor said.[3] Taylor became the highest selling country artist of 2008, just two short years after releasing her **debut** album.

◀ Taylor's music video for her song "Love Story" won a CMT Music Award in 2009.

▲ Kanye West interrupted Taylor's acceptance speech at the 2009 MTV Video Music Awards.

In 2009, Taylor reached another milestone. By this time, Taylor was accustomed to standing on stage with thousands of eyes on her. But it felt like a dream when she was handed the MTV Video Music Award (VMA) for Best Female Music Video. Her music video "You Belong with Me" had earned her the award. She was the first country music artist to win a VMA.

Taylor began her acceptance speech, but she never finished it. "I always dreamed about what it would be like to maybe win one of these someday, but I never actually thought it would have happened," Taylor said to the crowd.[4] She gazed at her award as the microphone was ripped from her hand by rapper Kanye West.

West declared that Beyoncé should have won the award. He shoved the microphone back at Taylor and quickly left the stage. The crowed exploded with noise. Taylor stood speechless, staring at her award. However, Taylor wasn't about to let one rapper's opinion stop her from making music. She was proud of herself for winning the VMA. And Taylor wondered if it was time to step into another music **genre**.

> "I have this really high priority on happiness and finding something to be happy about."[5]
>
> —*Taylor Swift*

Chapter 4

CROSSOVER TALENT

Taylor's cheeks were flushed, and she was out of breath from singing and dancing for her new music video. It was a lot of work but also a lot of fun. She got to dress up in a ballerina outfit, hip-hop clothing, and even a cheerleader's uniform. The song was bouncy, a little goofy, and unlike anything she'd released before. It was definitely not a country song. Taylor's newest hit song was titled "Shake It Off." Taylor had continued to release albums that were loaded with hits. She had also continued to gain popularity beyond country music fans. Her albums *Speak Now* and *Red* had been successful on both the country and pop charts. In 2014, Taylor released her fifth studio album, *1989*.

◀ Taylor's album *1989* won her many awards at the Billboard Music Awards in 2015.

▲ **Taylor's first pop album was an immediate success.**

Her songs branched out from the country music rhythms. She was ready to take the pop world by storm. *1989*'s first single, "Shake It Off," was an anthem for anyone who felt bullied. With an entertaining video to go along with the song, Taylor's first true attempt at pop music was a huge success. "Shake It Off" was the most popular song of 2015.

It appears there is nothing Taylor can't accomplish. She started out as a young girl, desperate for her music to be recognized. She grew into a superstar, pop music **diva**, actress, and even fashion cover model. Today, Taylor continues to follow her passion for songwriting and making music.

THINK ABOUT IT

- Taylor writes many of her songs about things that have happened in her life. Would you be brave enough to let the world hear about your experiences and disappointments?
- Taylor constantly deals with critics. How would you handle someone saying that what you do is bad?
- With her album *1989*, Taylor shifted from country to pop music. Do you think it would be more difficult to cross over to a different music genre or to keep creating new music in one genre?

GLOSSARY

acoustic (uh-KOO-stik): Acoustic music is music that is not electrically amplified. Taylor grabbed her guitar and played an acoustic version of her favorite song.

album (AL-buhm): An album is a collection of music on a CD or record. Taylor released her first album in 2006.

debut (day-BYOO): A debut is a first public appearance or performance. Taylor's debut album came out in 2006.

demo (DEM-oh): A demo is music that is recorded to introduce the performer to others. Taylor made a demo in hopes of getting a record deal.

diva (DEE-vah): A diva is a glamorous and successful female singer. Taylor became a pop diva after her album *1989*.

genre (ZHAHN-ruh): Genre is a category of music characterized by a particular style. Taylor stepped into the pop music genre.

single (SING-guhl): A single is a recording and/or popular release of a single song. Taylor released her single "Shake It Off" in 2014.

SOURCE NOTES

1. Edward Morris. "When She Thinks 'Tim McGraw,' Taylor Swift Savors Payoff." *CMT News*. Viacom International Inc., 1 Dec. 2006. Web. 17 Feb. 2017.

2. Lauren Waterman. "Swift Ascent." *TeenVogue*. Condé Nast, 25 Jan. 2009. Web. 17 Feb. 2017.

3. Kara Warner. "Taylor Swift Shares Her 'Quirky' Songwriting Process for 'Storytellers.'" *MTV News*. Viacom International, Inc., 17 Oct. 2012. Web. 17 Feb. 2017.

4. Daniel Kreps. "Kayne West Storms the VMAs Stage During Taylor Swift's Speech." *Rolling Stone*. Rolling Stone, 13 Sept. 2009. Web. 17 Feb. 2017.

5. Sharon Clott Kanter. "InStyle's June Cover Girl Is…Taylor Swift!" *InStyle*. Time Inc., 17 May 2011. Web. 17 Feb. 2017.

TO LEARN MORE

Books

Landau, Elaine. *Is the Guitar for You?* Minneapolis, MN: Lerner, 2011.

Morreale, Marie. *Taylor Swift: Born to Sing!* New York, NY: Children's Press, 2017.

Newkey-Burden, Chas. *Taylor Swift Unauthorised: The Whole Story.* London, England: Harper, 2014.

Web Sites

Visit our Web site for links about Taylor Swift: childsworld.com/links

Note to Parents, Teachers, and Librarians: We routinely verify our Web links to make sure they are safe and active sites. So encourage your readers to check them out!

INDEX

Academy of Country Music Awards, 12–13

Big Machine Records, 9

Country Music Association, 13

dancing, 7, 19

demo, 8

Fearless (album), 15

guitar, 9, 13

lyrics, 7, 15

MTV Video Music Awards, 16–17

music charts, 15, 19

music industry, 8, 13

Nashville, 8–9

1989 (album), 19–20

record deal, 8–9

"Shake It Off," 19–21

singing, 7–9, 12–13, 19

Songwriter's Showcase, 9

songwriting, 9, 11, 13, 15, 21

Taylor Swift (album), 12

West, Kanye, 17